DESIGN HAPPY

COLORFUL HOMES FOR THE MODERN FAMILY

BETSY WENTZ
Foreword by TORI MELLOTT

Gibbs Smith

CONTENTS

FOREWORD

"Matchy-matchy" is probably not what comes to mind when searching for words to describe Betsy Wentz's interiors. And yet it is precisely what comes to my mind.

When I first met Betsy, two things happened. First, I was mesmerized and awestruck by her energy and unflinching zest for life. When Betsy walks into a room, she brings with her a few impressive things. On the face of it, she brings pure glamour. With her perfectly coiffed, blonde bob swaying from side to side, and no doubt some fabulous dress, Betsy radiates the kind of mysterious allure that is rare these days. She is tasteful yet fiery, like an old Hollywood movie star who comes back with clever quips for sassy reporters. Betsy also brings with her the best, brightest, and happiest sunshine; it's as if the sun itself has found its way through the door and has charmed every guest in the room with its warm and welcoming aura. She also brings a breezy lightness. Like an artful magician, she offsets the intensity of her megawatt brilliance with a relaxed buoyancy—she keeps things light and fun and easy. Most notably, Betsy brings immeasurable passion to everything she does. She is wildly passionate about design, her family, her community, and her friends. Her energy is at once intense and effortless. She is bold but never brazen, she is jaunty without it being off-putting, and she celebrates the beauty of design without it feeling disingenuous. People who possess these rare and remarkable qualities always inspire me; Betsy is one of them.

After reading how she is a study in opposites, you might be wondering how the matchy-matchy part comes into play. You see, Betsy's interiors match her personality precisely; they are the literal manifestation of her soul. Her interiors are warm, energetic, and full of life. They are vibrant, rich, and maintain a cheerful blend of color, pattern, and texture. And yet they are also livable, classic, and true. She tempers and pacifies her bold fusion of design with a soothing air of glassy coolness. While she's careful to include her clients' wants and needs, Betsy infuses and imbues each room with her signature touch. As you turn the pages of this book and study its contents, you'll not only notice the brilliant rooms and magnetic photographs, but you'll also start to know the person, Betsy Wentz, on a much deeper plane, for it's her shining personality that pops from every page.

I mentioned two things happened to me when I met Betsy Wentz, and the second is that I made an instantaneous friend. Who doesn't want to be friends with someone who can so elegantly possess all those impressive attributes without ever making anyone else feel small? In fact, Betsy makes it a point to lift others up and celebrate the beauty and accomplishments of those around her. It has been fun and thrilling to watch Betsy's career skyrocket over the last several years, and I know this book is just the beginning. I hope you enjoy getting to know Betsy and her enchanting designs as much as I have, and maybe if you already know her or are lucky enough to meet her one day, you'll see what I mean when I say she's the perfect matchy-matchy for rooms and people alike.

—TORI MELLOTT
STYLE DIRECTOR AT F. SCHUMACHER AND *FREDERIC* MAGAZINE

INTRODUCTION

I was probably six years old when I started tagging along with my mom, Kay, to work. Although it was just a hobby, my mom had amassed an entire interior design showroom above the carriage house of our Pittsburgh-area home. The small space was packed wall to wall with fabrics and wallpapers. Most Tuesdays and Thursdays her shop was open, and I'd sit on the floor and sort fabrics. Sometimes I'd go with her to see clients or even take a trip to the New York Design Center. Those days were magical to me.

If you had told me then that I would somehow blend my early career training as a behavioral psychologist with that time spent with my mom into a successful interior design business and a shop of my own, I would never have believed it. But that's exactly what happened.

I started my career in counseling, earning a master's degree and working in the mental health field for several years. I learned so much about people, which proved to be very helpful when I left the therapy world and joined my mom's design business. Kay was an incredible teacher, a visionary, and a huge influence on who I am and what I do today. Those years working together and developing my design aesthetic were the greatest gift. We didn't always agree, but Kay taught me how to mix patterns, be unafraid of color, and, most importantly, how to communicate and develop relationships with clients. My mom would always say, "You have to discover something your client loves. Design is about finding the happy."

That is how I begin every project: looking for what makes my client happy. I say, "Let's find something you love—whether it's a rug, a fabric, a wallpaper, or a piece of artwork." Each project then unfolds into an authentic, unique story and a reflection of the person or family who lives there.

This book shares the decisions I consider together with my clients when designing each aspect of a house. It includes color studies, inspirational images of the spaces, and practical advice for anyone who might face the same challenges I did.

Today, I am blessed to have an amazing husband who helps me balance four very active children, two dogs, both our extended families, and my design career. I am rewarded every day with a family I love, a job I'm passionate about, a dedicated team I couldn't live without, and, most importantly, clients and friends whose lives and homes I get to help make happy places to be. I'm so excited to share some of my favorite projects with you, and I hope the advice and tips I pass along help you make your home beautiful, functional, and full of your own joy. This book was born out of a desire to honor my mom, who continues to inspire me every day. I dedicate it to her memory.

ARLINGTON

THE RIGHT BALANCE

Good design is all about form and function. I'm always trying to combine the two to discover the right balance for the clients. This project was particularly challenging; with a family of eight and a few pets, the homeowners wanted casual, colorful, and functional. When the clients bought an older stone house, they knew that they wanted to update the kitchen and add on a few more rooms to accommodate their large family. We made a master plan for renovation while starting right away on furnishings and decorations for the existing space.

BENJAMIN MOORE PAINT COLORS, FROM TOP: Old Glory 811, Kiwi 544, Jupiter Glow 021, Rendezvous Bay 726, Hale Navy HC-154, Claret Rose 2008-20.

As with most older homes, there were some quirky features that we had to work around (think radiators and masonry walls). The living room was particularly challenging as it has three doorways leading from the hall, the study, and the kitchen. The room is long and narrow as well, which is always tricky when considering the most functional floor plan. We decided on two separate seating areas to allow a walkway to the husband's study.

The inspiration for this room was the floral drapery with shades of blue and a hint of citron. We pulled the peacock-blue shade out for the tone-on-tone wallpaper and a rich teal color for the velvet lounge chairs. A love seat in pale gray and occasional chairs in a small neutral pattern sit on a neutral geometric wool rug that acts to ground the room and unite the two seating areas. Large, colorful artwork jumps off the walls, and we hung vintage plates over the fireplace to provide interest.

ABOVE: A small study is nestled just off the formal living room. The apple green grass cloth wallpaper paired with classic plaid draperies making this the perfect spot to escape.

OPPOSITE: A dark, silky rug anchors the large wood dining table, which is surrounded by dining chairs upholstered in a colorful chevron pattern. (They're also performance fabric, making them spill resistant.) A black-and-white gallery wall lends itself to the high contrast nature of the room.

The kitchen was reworked to include new backsplash tile, cabinets, and countertops. A large center island was key to being able to seat all six kids and was the perfect spot to showcase two oversize, custom-colored pendants. We intentionally left lots of open floor space for traffic flow in the kitchen, which also allowed the opportunity to have some fun with vintage rugs and runners.

This mom of six needed a home base in the kitchen, so we designed a custom, built-in desk with file drawers to keep her organized.

OPPOSITE BELOW: One of my favorite treatments—cork covered in decorative mica paper—offers a serious upgrade to the traditional corkboard, serving as a place to display calendars, party invitations, and sports schedules.

PRO TIP

A good strategy for large-family dining is to use a bench in lieu of chairs, because you can squeeze more people in when necessary.

Just off the kitchen, the breakfast room has French doors leading to the back patio. Floor-to-ceiling windows flood the space with light and provide the perfect opportunity to use a dark blue wallpaper for contrast. We dressed the windows in a print with various shades of blue and used a polypropylene outdoor rug to protect the floors from frequent dog traffic.

OPPOSITE: A large custom-colored large lantern-style light fixture anchors the large dining table and dining benches.

ABOVE: We added a console to provide a spot for buffet-style serving and a large round mirror to reflect all the light in the room.

The screened-in porch boasts a fabulous, wood-burning stone fireplace and views to the backyard. A poly rug was chosen for durability. A large sectional in navy blue performance fabric provides more than enough seating for a crowd, and bright, patterned pillows finish the room.

DESIGN LESSON

Seating for a Family Room

The family room is a gathering space for everything from TV watching to socializing and game playing. As a result, it's the room where you'll want to get the most seating possible. Allow 24 inches per person to sit—whether on a sofa, love seat, chair, or bench.

A sectional is almost always the best way to maximize seating in a room. I love them for families with children.

Sectionals are flexible and come in many different shapes and sizes. To find the perfect size and shape for you, I recommend you start with the sectional size. One easy way to do this is to take blue painter's tape and mark off the dimensions on the floor. This will give you a visual of the exact length and depth the furniture piece will take up in your room.

The primary gathering spot for the family is the sunken family room, just off the kitchen. When considering the floor plan, we needed to be sure the furniture could seat at least ten people at any given time, so we designed a custom sectional. The clients fell in love with a vibrant, stylized, multicolored floral for the drapery, which gave us a lot of colors to work with.

Neutral textured wallpaper and a solid performance fabric on the sectional provide the base. Bright pillows and Lucite benches with colorful seats add pops of energy. A large coffee table is a spot for the family to play games.

ABOVE RIGHT: The bookcases were modernized by adding orange pussy willow–patterned wallpaper to the backs and oversize knobs to the doors. These are examples of small details that make this family home special.

ABOVE LEFT AND RIGHT: The main bedroom is just at the top of the front steps. Like the rest of the house, this space had great light and lots of windows. We carried the coral and soft blue shades from downstairs in the form of embroidered floral drapery, occasional chairs, and a lush velvet bench at the foot of the custom bed. Neutral textured paper serves as a backdrop for the couple's colorful artwork.

OPPOSITE: The primary bath was small, but a minor renovation to the space made it more functional and appealing. An otherwise ordinary room was made special with a playful, beaded chandelier and a colorful Roman shade that pulls all the colors from the bedroom.

PRO TIP:

Don't be afraid to make highly functional spaces beautiful—we spend so much time there!

Treat your closets and stairways like any room in your house. Add wallpaper and window treatments to make them happy spaces too.

OPPOSITE: The mudroom is the primary entrance for family and friends, so the couple really wanted something fun. A fiery red textured wallpaper is complemented by a one-of-a-kind vintage runner with the same color tones. These vintage rugs are my favorite because they offer both color and durability. Contrary to popular belief, most vintage rugs are indestructible and colorfast. Lighting is key in this space, so we selected a high-wattage fixture in a soft blue to match the abstract pattern in the Roman shades.

ABOVE RIGHT: A textured wallpaper, striped wool carpet, and a roman shade dress up the primary closet.

BELOW RIGHT: The back stairwell got multicolored feather wallpaper and an oversize coco bead chandelier.

BLACKWOOD FARM

MODERN FARM LIVING

This project was a rare opportunity to start from scratch and build from the ground up. Former clients and dear friends had been yearning to find a large piece of land to fulfill a lifelong dream of living on a farm. A fifty-acre lot in Indiana County, Pennsylvania, proved to be the perfect location to build their dream farmhouse, raise chickens, and start a second career as local flower farmers.

I worked closely with the homeowners and their architects at Shea & Simone to design a house that balanced both traditional and modern design. The interior of the main house is more traditionally designed, with heavier crown molding, twelve-foot ceilings, and a curved staircase. Moving to the back of the house, the heavier architectural details give way to more modern and streamlined spaces, including a retractable window wall and a two-story screened-in porch.

BENJAMIN MOORE PAINT COLORS, FROM TOP: Edgecomb Gray HC-173, Palace Blue CW -605, Timber Wolf 1600, Coral Dust 2173-50, Charcoal Slate HC 178, Navajo White OC- 95.

The floor plan here was a bit tricky, as we had a staircase, a piano, and multiple windows to work around. A chair with a narrow silhouette balanced by the plant's foliage is the perfect fit.

ABOVE: This new build looks like an old Bucks County farmhouse. To achieve the look of having been added to over time, the home's exterior is a mix of reclaimed stone from a regional quarry and barn woods from Pennsylvania and Ohio barns.

OPPOSITE: A sprawling, Southern-style front porch—punctuated with a door in robin's-egg blue—welcomes you into the foyer. The entry doubles as a hallway that connects the open living room on the right and the dining room on the left (see pages 32–35).

PRO TIP

Float sculptural
elements or artwork
to create separate
areas in a
large space.

The homeowners wanted the living room to feel like a special spot, so it is elevated and set apart from the entry and dining room by three steps and flanked by a set of pillars that were designed to display matching sculptures by artist Andrianna Shamaris. The goal in this space was a quiet, neutral feel. We repeated the exterior stone on the wood-burning fireplace, which acts as the centerpiece of the room. We opted for a cowhide rug, so as not to cover too much of the gorgeous, wide-plank, natural

wood floors, and we punctuated with touches of black, white, and lilac. A sofa and an assortment of occasional chairs keep the conversation area close while allowing a nice traffic flow.

ABOVE RIGHT: Corners and nooks of rooms can be made special by clustering plants, accessories, and collectibles.

The dining room began with a fantastic ikat stripe wallpaper that grounds the wood beams and carries over the black-and-cream palette from the living room. A very large rug was needed to accommodate an heirloom dining table and chairs. We went with a dark graphic pattern to contrast the light floors and refreshed the dining chairs with an aubergine velvet.

The couple are both passionate cooks who wanted a huge area to do their thing. The kitchen needed to be highly functional but also provide a comfortable place for friends and family to gather. The two long islands, one for prep work and another for serving, have stools on one side so the person cooking can be part of the conversation. A custom steel pot rack with leather straps is both functional and a focal point of the prep island. Extra-thick Danby marble countertops, a handmade turquoise tile backsplash, and antique mirror glass behind the shelves make this kitchen one of a kind.

OPPOSITE: The custom pot rack and David Weeks lighting adorn the two large islands, creating balance for the space.

ABOVE: People are often afraid to have rugs and "real" furniture in their kitchens, but I find it one of the most effective ways to create warmth and coziness. A seating arrangement with four large swivel chairs in front of the fireplace is anchored by a one-of-a-kind silk rug of recycled saris.

OPPOSITE: The glass doors open to a screened-in fireplace and porch area that the family uses heavily. The idea was to have the space unfold toward the exterior. We treated it as a living room, with sofas, lounge chairs, and a large coffee table for entertaining.

ABOVE: Just off the kitchen is a second staircase, where we combined antique mirror glass, reclaimed barn wood, and wallpaper to add dimension.

OPPOSITE: The back staircase ascending from the kitchen leads directly into the main suite, where the couple wanted plenty of room to spread out. We began in the large entry with lounge chairs and a pair of antique chests that belonged to the owner's grandmother. New matching mirrors and light fixtures reflect the light from the beaded wallpaper, while reclaimed barn wood echoes the rustic style of the rest of the home.

ABOVE: In contrast to the heaviness of the wood, abstract watercolor wallpaper in a soft palette creates an ethereal feel in the sleeping area. A custom shag rug and neutral draperies leave the space feeling casual and inviting.

A deck connects the main bedroom to a bonus guest area above the garage. Here we created a private seating area that allows a panoramic view of the property.

DESIGN LESSON

Outdoor Spaces

Like any other room in your house, your outdoor space should have a clear purpose and be outfitted with all the elements to achieve it.

- If you have a large outdoor space, breaking it into smaller segments is a good idea. You can use furniture to delineate seating and dining areas and separate small resting spots with walkways. Remember, strategic flow still applies here.

- In lieu of walls, consider using plants and vegetation to divide the spaces visually and physically.

- When designing your outdoor space, I recommend starting with an overall plan. You don't have to execute it all at once, but a good design will ensure the spaces and pathways flow well. You can implement the plan in logical and affordable stages.

BUNKER HILL

A HOME FOR ALL CREATURES

Bunker Hill is one of the oldest and most beautiful homes in Sewickley Heights, Pennsylvania. It is a stately stone residence that overlooks the sixth fairway of the Allegheny Country Club. When some longtime friends told me that they were purchasing the house, I was thrilled! As with most historic homes, there was much to do before we could get to the fun part. After a series of renovations—including a kitchen remodel and various bedroom additions—the house was ready for the good stuff! What followed was a long journey combining the homeowners' family antiques with new pieces that we selected together.

BENJAMIN MOORE PAINT COLORS, FROM TOP: Green Bay 2045-10, White Dove OC-17, Dark Teal 2053-20, Damask Yellow CW400, Victoriana 1263, Powell Gray CW665.

Above all else, this is a family house. The couple has three children and three large golden retrievers. The kitchen's French doors are often left open during the day for the dogs and kids to run in and out. I've had the privilege of spending quite a bit of time as a guest in this house and it was not uncommon to have muddy dogs running through any room. So, we needed to create comfortable and functional spaces that were also beautiful.

We were able to incorporate many works of art, accessories, and furniture pieces that had belonged to family members, which always makes a project more interesting.

We tackled the formal living room first—although no space in this house is truly formal. The family wanted to keep this room light and bright. To bring the outdoors inside, we selected a neutral palette except for the oversize custom ottoman, which is covered in a colorful, large-scale plaid.

The floor plan in this room proved to be very challenging, as we were working with a fireplace, five doorways, and a full-size piano. It's important to consider not only what will look the best, but how the room will function. In this case, the room serves as more of a gathering space for special occasions. The couple really wanted to be able to seat many family members around the fireplace. To accommodate this, we landed on a design with two matching custom sofas facing one another. We finished off the seating arrangement with a leather love seat that had belonged to the wife's father and held a lot of sentimental value for her.

A vintage record player and the homeowners' record collection give the game room personality.

During initial renovations, the homeowners replaced the floor in the game room with a beautiful redbrick in a herringbone pattern. The room has a pool table and several other games, but they also wanted to have a place to lounge. To offer optimal seating in the small corner, I designed a custom sectional to fit the space.

The game room has windows running around two sides of it. While there was plenty of light, the odd window positioning would have made drapery difficult. Instead, we found our inspiration for color in the fabrics on the sectional and a vintage rug that I found in Palm Beach.

The dining room, like the other spaces of the house, is informal. Since it's located in the high-traffic area between the kitchen and the game room, it has to be practical. The old farm table and chairs have been in the family for a long time and double as a homework table for kids. Still, every dining room needs a touch of glam. So, we added silver metallic, grass cloth–textured paper to the walls, which provides a neutral but bright back-drop for the couple's favorite work of art—a simple barn scene with a tangerine-colored background.

The wood-burning fireplace makes this an irresistible spot to curl up with a book or a movie.

Just past the dining room is the coziest nook in all of Bunker Hill. The den previously had old pine wood cladding all the walls and bookcases. While charming, it made the room very dark. So, we opted to paint the walls, bookcases, and trim a rich teal color.

Since this is the most informal space in the house and the dogs tend to lounge in here, we chose a weathered leather sectional to hide everything from dog hair to popcorn. Any wear also just adds to the furniture's patina. We selected a drapery to contrast with the walls and a bright vintage rug for a pop of color.

The map reads:

MANHATTAN
HUDSON RIVER
NEW JERSEY
RIVERSIDE PARK
MORNINGSIDE HEIGHTS
HAMILTON HEIGHTS
UPPER WEST SIDE
HELL'S KITCHEN
MIDTOWN
TIMES SQUARE
CENTRAL PARK
HARLEM
CHEL SEA
GREEN WICH VILLAGE
GARMENT DISTRICT
SOHO
UPPER EAST SIDE
YORK VILLE
EAST HARLEM
FINANCIAL DISTRICT
TRIBECA
EAST VILLAGE
GRAMERCY
MURRAY HILL
MIDTOWN EAST
CHINA TOWN
LITTLE ITALY
BRONX
LOWER EAST SIDE
ALPHABET CITY
STUYVESANT TOWN
BROOKLYN
EAST RIVER
QUEENS

S
Bunker Hill

The kitchen is the heart and soul of this house. It's where all the family meals and conversations take place. The French doors lead out to the covered patio, which also serves as a secondary "room" and often doubles as a gathering space when the weather is good. When renovating the kitchen, the homeowners decided to bump out the existing space to add seating to the extra-large center island. A custom hood anchors the main space, and the classic white subway tile is timeless.

RIGHT: We created additional seating in a small corner by building an upholstered banquette.

DESIGN LESSON

Functional Can Be Beautiful

In a busy house with kids and pets, practicality is almost always a high priority. Being functional does not mean something has to be utilitarian and ugly, though. Here are some easy ways to make basic spaces look good and work well.

- **Use performance and/or outdoor fabrics** inside to ensure durability. These fabrics have been treated to be stain resistant and can be easily wiped down when there are spills.

- Consider using **vegetable-dyed vintage rugs** in high traffic areas, as they hide a multitude of sins!

- **Vinyl that looks like leather** is a great option for barstools, other seating, and ottomans, where kids often make messes. It is durable, wipeable, and cleans up easily.

- I almost always recommend **vinyl wallpaper**, especially in hallways and bathrooms. It provides texture, is completely wipeable, and is much more durable than paint.

The mudroom, meanwhile, needed to be all function in this house with three large dogs! The homeowners selected a heavy-duty dark tile in the sunken mudroom with shiplap walls and a reclaimed-wood ceiling. Industrial pendant lights ground the center island, which was designed to hold off-season clothing and pet supplies. We added some eye-catching vintage runners for color and a very special piece of artwork by Andrew Moser.

The main bedroom was one of the very last things we designed in this house. It required an extensive renovation and reconfiguration of an existing bathroom to create a main bath. One result of this renovation was a peaked ceiling, which became the highlight of the room. Small windows posed a bit of a challenge in how to treat them while keeping the room light and bright. We added white shiplap on the peaked ceiling to maintain the lightness and keep the room looking fresh. A textured wallpaper draws the eye outward.

ABOVE: We painted the walls an azure blue and hung a soft lilac macramé tapestry over the bed to personalize this room for a teenage girl.

CAMPBELL CREEK

HOUSE MEETS COLOR

In a color-loving designer's own home, there's no such thing as too much pattern.

My own Sewickley, Pennsylvania, home is a convergence of all my favorite design lessons: color, pattern, modern-meets-traditional, and, with four busy kids, a whole lot of functionality. The way we landed on this house, though, was a bit of a surprise. We had just finished renovating another house. I was out jogging and saw a "For Sale" sign. I've lived in this area my whole life and had never noticed this property. So, I ran up the driveway, and there was a very ordinary 1970s structure—but it was on a beautiful lot. I fell in love with the piece of land, and we purchased it. After the Great Recession hit, though, we put off renovations, and this allowed us time to live in the home and see what we needed to change. We finally moved in the night we had our youngest daughter, Marlowe.

BENJAMIN MOORE PAINT COLORS, FROM TOP: Vermilion 2002-10, Downpour Blue 2063-20, Simply White 2143-70, Crocus 1404, Vine Green 2034-20, Royal Fuchsia 2078-30.

My kids all play sports and are constantly in and out of the house's side door. To contain all their gear, I designed floor-to-ceiling lockers, each covered in a different shade of glossy paint. This truly practical element becomes like a piece of art, adding a profusion of color that isn't often seen in modern homes.

DESIGN LESSON
Fabrics Make the Space

One of the best ways to personalize your home is through fabrics. Here are the best ways:

Start with drapery. Even if you don't need the drapery for function, fabric panels and/or Roman shade valances are a great way to add color and pattern to your space and to lend softness and warmth. This fabric will often provide a starting point for selecting all the other colors in the room. When choosing drapery fabric, look for a larger scale pattern with multiple colors; this will give you more options for other pieces in the room.

Then add upholstery. Look at the largest piece of upholstered furniture in the room. Think of it as your base layer—it's the pair of blue jeans in the room. The supporting pieces of upholstery can have smaller scale patterns, like a geometric or an animal print.

Layer in accessories. Pillows are an inexpensive and simple way to create excitement with colors, patterns, and textures.

Since the kitchen is open to the dining area (and looks out to the woodsy surroundings), I wanted to anchor the room with some wood. I worked with my cabinetmaker to create the paneled cabinets, as well as several island blocks for different purposes. There's an eat-in island with warm wood siding, a central island for cooking (with a pop of lacquer that connects back to the lockers), and a desk so I can work from the center of the home.

PRO TIP

By placing the sink
in the island, you can
avoid having your
back to those sitting
at the island.

To maximize views to the outside, I decided not to go
for upper cabinets on the far side of the kitchen.

Whenever possible, I like to place the primary kitchen sink in the island. I find, as a busy mom of four myself, I spend 80 percent of my time at the sink doing dishes, washing fruits and vegetables, and prepping meals.

The dining area is my favorite little spot in the house. We had our architect bump out a glass box to mirror the one at the formal front entrance then added a live-edge table for an organic balance to all that glass and the concrete floor. This was basically a family compromise: we wanted a clean, modern house, but we also needed it to be warm and kid friendly.

Right off the kitchen and dining area is where our family hangs out. I chose a large sectional to fit the whole family and act as a neutral backdrop to the colorful elements, like armchairs, pillows, and a red lantern from Urban Electric whose glossy finish ties back to the lockers across the space.

Since our more formal living room doesn't get as much use as some of the central spaces, I decided to go bold and give this room at the back of the house a fun pop. Even though we don't go into this room all the time, we can see it through the other spaces. I used a graphic tree wallpaper and accented with tons of bold colors pulled from other rooms in the house.

Not many men have a lavender study, but my husband was game for this color, which adds freshness to the 1970s room. I know it might seem a little crazy to have all these patterns, but these are decisions I do not make lightly. Many edits and revisions go into creating a perfect mix.

OPPOSITE AND ABOVE: The graphic rug connects the room's elements, from bold green chairs to tie-dyed drapery, to my children's framed artwork.

The main entry was designed as a glass "box" to mirror the larger dining area just off the kitchen on the back side of the house.

OPPOSITE: At the top of the main entry stairs and outside of all the bedrooms is a centrally located study and lounge area. It serves as another spot for kids to both gather and get away from the crowd when needed.

PRO TIP

A corkboard wall allows kids to be the designers of their own rooms without breaking the budget or ruining the drywall.

Marlowe
Campbell Wentz

Framed kids' artwork and an organic wood bench help make the bathroom feel cozy.

I designed my only daughter's room while I was pregnant with her; I wanted it to be girly but also be able to grow with her. I selected my favorite shade of bubblegum-pink vinyl wallcovering and paired it with a Trina Turk chevron fabric for the drapery. The wall behind her bed is wallpaper over corkboard, so she can hang anything she wants with push pins.

I wanted the kids' bathroom to be colorful and fun while keeping it gender neutral. To create interest, I used a high-contrast geometric tile for the floor. A bright, striped-linen, Roman shade and a turquoise vinyl wallpaper finish off the space.

PRO TIP

Lighting design in a bedroom is essential. It's the only room where you transition from wake to sleep, sleep to wake, and everything in between. Bedrooms should have a mix of lighting, including overhead, accent, and task.

Our main bedroom is probably the visually quietest room in the house; I love how it acts as a calm oasis. Since some of the most dramatic windows in the house are at the corner of this bedroom, I started with the drapery. I loved the silver and wanted it to be a little bit calmer in here so we could have that treetop feeling. The art above the bed from Porter Teleo carries on the hues from the drapery.

Our bathroom has a dreamy soaking tub and is complete with a coffee bar and mini fridge for bath-time espresso—or Champagne!

DOGWOOD

SOMETHING OLD IS NEW AGAIN

I was watching my son's game when one of my fellow soccer moms mentioned they had recently purchased a 1970s ranch-style house in the area. The house was in a great location but had not been touched in years. They had just started a major renovation with an addition and immediately felt overwhelmed by all the decisions. Over the course of nine months, we worked closely to renovate and expand this house to ensure that the spaces would flow and be functional for the family of four.

When you take on a renovation, one of the biggest decisions is where to prioritize the budget. In the long run, a designer can save money by helping clients avoid mistakes. Most of the original house was renovated and updated. A hallway and staircase were added to connect the main house to a second-floor, two-bedroom–one bathroom addition. The result was an overhaul with no shortage of architectural style and personal flair. As a bonus, the homeowners love color and wanted me to help them express that throughout the interior—which is something I love to do!

BENJAMIN MOORE PAINT COLORS, FROM TOP: Yellow Tone 370, Gypsy Rose 1327, Kensington Blue 840, Juniper 2048-20, Brown Sugar 2112-20, Rose Blush 037.

An abstract rug complements the drapery and custom, citron-painted sconces.

The dining room is smack dab in the middle of the linear house and offers incredible views of the town through a new picture window that was added during the renovation. The couple wanted a live-edge dining table, so that was one of our first purchases. We also chose a two-globe light fixture to hang from the newly vaulted ceiling. The color story started with the playful drapery fabric, which we pulled from for the dark teal dining chairs.

The kitchen area had its limitations, as it was part of the original structure and required us to leave the low ceiling height. To open the space, we added several windows on the back wall then placed an oversize island in the center to provide ample prep surface and an additional spot to eat. The backsplash tile runs all the way to the ceiling, creating a cohesive feel.

The island base was painted blue to tie in the colors from the dining room, while custom, pink-patterned stools add a dose of whimsy.

OPPOSITE: The formal front entry is off the dining room. Although small, it's full of life with a fuchsia and coral color scheme, an enchanting vintage cabinet, and a large modern artwork.

ABOVE: The powder room is tucked just off the entry. A geometric purple, citron, and blue wallpaper wraps the walls, while custom electric-blue sconces light the small but super-fun space.

The living room mirrors the vaulted ceiling and picture window from the dining room, offering a similar view to the village below. We took advantage of the light streaming into the space by utilizing a patterned grass cloth with a dark ground and a hint of metallic, creating a moody backdrop for the ombré drapery and bright yellow accents.

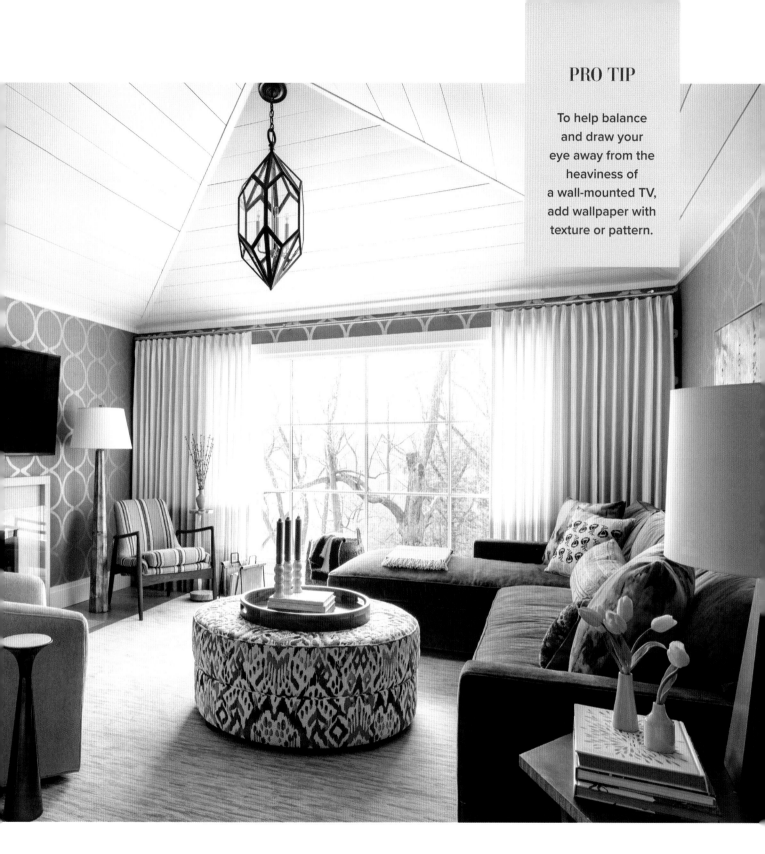

PRO TIP

To help balance
and draw your
eye away from the
heaviness of
a wall-mounted TV,
add wallpaper with
texture or pattern.

My favorite piece in the room is undoubtedly the round ottoman
that we designed in a dynamic ikat print, showcasing all the
colors of the house. I almost always prefer an ottoman to a
table, both for looks and comfort.

We used a colorful vintage rug in the long hallway approaching the main suite to introduce the suite's rich color palette. My client fell in love with a deep shade of cocoa wallpaper with a subtle stripe. The vaulted ceiling and multiple windows allowed us to use this deep shade while keeping the space light and fresh. To introduce some femininity to the strong backdrop, we chose a solid blush cotton sateen for all the draperies. The combination is soothing and alluring.

We hung a collection of handmade straw discs in a random pattern to fill the space above the bed. I just love the way they pop off the dark ground.

DESIGN LESSON

Renovation Advice

Everyone starts with very high expectations when starting a remodel, especially at the beginning. Inevitably, there will be setbacks and many unhappy surprises along the way. Keeping these things in mind will help reduce your stress when things come up:

- The timeline is almost always unrealistic.

- The budget is probably the biggest concern of most remodelers, and people seriously under-estimate how much a home renovation will cost—even before the surprises pop up. Have the hard conversations first to set a realistic budget and understand that you may need to work in phases. This will save heartache later when the design may have to be sacrificed given changes in construction or costs. It's good to be flexible but also to establish a clear game plan.

- Be Realistic. You can fall in love with a magazine image depicting floor-to-ceiling French doors with the Pacific Ocean in the background, but if you live in Philadelphia, that will never be your reality! The name of the game is using what you have to your advantage. Focus on the strengths of your space and try to play them up while keeping your mind open to unexpected, on-the-fly options that may present themselves.

- Know what you want. I always recommend living in a space before renovating. Your goals for the home can change drastically once you've utilized the space and figured out how it functions for you.

- Prioritize what is most important to you and your family. Most of us cannot do everything that we want in a renovation, so we must pick and choose. Get the biggest bang for your buck in major spaces like kitchens and family rooms. Prioritize the spaces you spend the most time in.

- Make sure your renovation design flows with the current architecture of the house, especially if you are adding on. A good designer or architect will help you create a plan to enhance your spaces.

- Limit floor transitions where possible, as they can create a choppy look. A continuous material invites visual flow.

- To make a small space feel bigger, consider widening doorways. A trick for creating the illusion of space is to add mirrors where you can. The more flow and view you can create from one room to another, the larger the space will appear.

EVERGLADES

DREAM NEW BUILD

In 2016, I learned that one of my oldest clients and dear friends had purchased property on Palm Beach Island. They were building their dream house and wanted me to help. Architecture and craftsmanship were very important to them.

The clients were already working with Tom Kirchhoff of Kirchhoff Architects and had designed a Mediterranean Revival home. The attention to detail and meticulous woodwork in the home provided the perfect backdrop for our interior design scheme.

PAINT COLORS, FROM TOP: Farrow & Ball Pointing 2003, Farrow & Ball Borrowed Light 235, Benjamin Moore Symphony Blue 2060-10, Benjamin Moore Galapagos Turquoise 2057-20, Benjamin Moore Newburyport Blue HC-155, Benjamin Moore Skydive CSP-700.

The home's layout was dictated by the loggia. The homeowners wanted a seamless flow between indoors and outdoors, which we achieved by coordinating the color of fabrics, rugs, and accessories. They also wanted the house to reflect their love of the water, so we layered varying shades of blue, from robin's egg to ink.

The striking front hall boasts a handmade Moroccan tile design on the floor. A coordinating mosaic pattern snakes up the curved staircase on the risers. A pair of oversize chairs covered in an embroidered leaf print fabric flank the antique chest and welcome guests in the foyer. We layered a mix of antiques and new furniture throughout the home, which creates depth and adds to its charm.

OPPOSITE: Moroccan-inspired sconces and ceiling fixtures create drama in the front hall.

RIGHT: I love a round dining table. All seats face the center, so everyone can see each other and take part in the conversation.

The quatrefoil shapes in the ceiling and chandelier are hallmarks of architect Addison Mizner, who, in the 1920s defined the Palm Beach mansion style.

The dining room is the most formal room in the house. We selected a neutral, cream-colored silk wallcovering, which paired nicely with the traditional, hand-blocked patterned drapery. An exaggerated tweed on the curved-back dining chairs adds texture—and a cover for spills. Oversize antique mirror sconces give the room a little glam.

PRO TIP

Connect
architectural details
to other elements
in the room. In this
space, the lighting
and textile patterns
highlight the
ceiling design.

DESIGN LESSON

How to Layer Patterns, Colors, and Texture

The key to layering is to select items that are similar in color tone but different in pattern and scale. There needs to be a common thread that creates harmony. Not everything has to match, but everything needs to flow.

Something in the room needs to be neutral before you add color layers. This is where it's fun to mix in different textures in neutral colors for a strong background.

Typically, we try to stick with the same color family. For instance, if you're using the medium bright family of a color (see page 159), stay there. All those colors should have a similar feel. Throwing a pastel in with a bunch of medium brights can jump out and throw everything off.

A good place to start is with an inspiration fabric—something with several colors and an interesting pattern scale. From there, you can mix and match geometrics, florals, and everything in between.

The custom, curved, navy velvet sofa invites guests to linger in this charming living room.

To the right of the entry is the living room, which is by far the grandest room in the house. Vaulted ceilings in pecky cypress and an oversize light fixture set the tone for relaxation as well as casual entertaining. We wanted the relatively large space to have a cohesive feel, so we began with a custom room-size rug featuring a plume pattern in various shades of blue. With such a large room, furniture can often get lost, and we wanted to make sure everyone in the room could be part of the conversation. We grounded the room with one large sofa and rounded out the area with two different sets of chairs and a custom bench in front of the fireplace. While we kept the draperies light with a neutral sheer, we added playfulness with the upholstery on the chairs, mixing patterns and textures.

ABOVE: Ultimately, we landed on two separate seating arrangements in the family room, with a break between the rugs to fill the needs of dining and lounging in the same space.

OPPOSITE: We hung round, open pendant lights over the island to break up all the straight lines and angles.

The kitchen and family room areas are open to one another, which proved challenging for several reasons. The family room is open to the kitchen, the main suite hall, the living room, and, most importantly, the loggia, which leads outside to the pool. With so many openings and pathways, we needed to figure out a furniture arrangement that would be both functional and visually appealing. We settled on two identical, disc-shaped, semi-flush-mount chandeliers to simultaneously delineate and unite the spaces. The result is a fully usable and beautiful space.

ABOVE: The kitchen cabinetry was finished in a luscious shade of denim blue and is complemented with light marble countertops. We kept the counters consistent throughout but swapped in a textural cypress for the island base.

The hallway to the main bedroom suite is one of my favorite spots in the house. It's lined in custom, Moroccan-inspired cabinetry to house the homeowner's large wine collection. Gilded-framed art and an antique mirror turn what would otherwise be an overlooked passageway into a dramatic focal point. We designed a custom, twenty-two-foot runner to complete the space.

OPPOSITE ABOVE: The main bedroom had lots of windows, so the drapery was of high importance here. We chose a horizontal ikat silk stripe in various shades of blue. A custom rug and a settee covered in silvery blue velvet finish off the suite.

OPPOSITE BELOW: The main suite bath boasts his-and-hers sinks, toilets, and dressing areas. Custom vanity cabinets in the same vein as the main hallway complement the intricate tile pattern on the floor. The soft blue flows from the bath right into the bedroom.

The loggia, positioned in a central courtyard, is the heart of this home. As the main meeting point and the inspiration for the surrounding home layout, it needed to be functional and comfortable and, of course, beautiful. We selected pieces with deeper seats and used outdoor-approved fabrics. An oversize lantern in the center of the space makes it feel more like a room and less like a patio.

The outdoor space was designed with minimal hardscape. Instead, grass frames the simple pool shape. The signature Mediterranean revival–inspired quatrefoil design adorns wooden gates that greet guests at the entry of the private outdoor oasis, which is strategically located near the loggia.

One of the most inviting areas in the house, the loggia combines functionality and comfort with striking outdoor fabrics and extra-deep chairs and sofa for lounging.

MOSS TRAIL

MIDCENTURY REMIX

I was delighted to receive a call from a local realtor who had recently purchased a midcentury modern home in a nearby suburb. The house sits on a generous wooded lot and is striking with its bold black exterior and two-story glass entrance. The clients wanted to create a clean, modern entertainer's haven that was still family friendly. We planned a two-phase project of the first floor: phase one was to decorate the living room, dining room, and entry; phase two was to renovate the kitchen and decorate the adjoining family room and bar area. In the middle of the kitchen renovation, our clients learned a new baby was on the way, so we happily added "decorate a nursery" to our list.

The homeowners were initially reluctant to use any color. They had envisioned a monochromatic interior of grays and whites. Luckily, they trusted our design process and fell in love with a deep teal and charcoal tribal-pattern wallpaper and agreed to try it on a wall in their living room. The result was stunning, and it sparked a desire to add more color throughout the rest of the house. The clients are now true color converts.

BENJAMIN MOORE PAINT COLORS, FROM TOP: Midnight Navy 2067-10, Fields of Gold 203, Teal 2055-10, Coventry Gray HC 169, Rust 2175-30, Saybrook Sage HC 114.

A walnut- and glass-paneled door opens into a large entryway with a floating wood staircase. We opted to leave the midcentury staircase design intact and wrapped each step with wool carpet in a deep shade of pine.

A bright, multicolor vintage rug grounds the lower entry. A live-edge console and a round, blackened-iron mirror finish the space.

PRO TIP

In a vast space with
high ceilings, drop
multiple light fixtures
to create drama.

An abstract painting presides over the incredible gathering space.

The living room is undoubtedly the most architecturally impressive space in the house. The twenty-foot ceiling paired with an asymmetrical window inspired me to do something special here. I pictured a fabulous wallpaper on the back wall. The couple was initially afraid of any bold color—but when I proposed the teal-colored textured paper, they went for it. A modern, patterned sheer dressed the windows and we added pops of marigold and navy for an unusual but amazing color combo.

To draw the eye to the oversize, live-edge coffee table below, I designed a cluster of different-size globes in mercury glass that fits perfectly between the wood beams. The result is one of my all-time favorite rooms.

Just across the way, the dining room is sandwiched
between the kitchen and living room. The kitchen was
simultaneously being renovated, and we wanted to
use the same colors in all three spaces for visual flow.
Because the ceilings were lower here, we kept the walls
light, using a pale gray textured paper with a multicolor
horizontal stripe. A playful micro stripe in chili pepper
red, navy, and cream is stacked at the windows and sets
the color story for the neighboring kitchen.

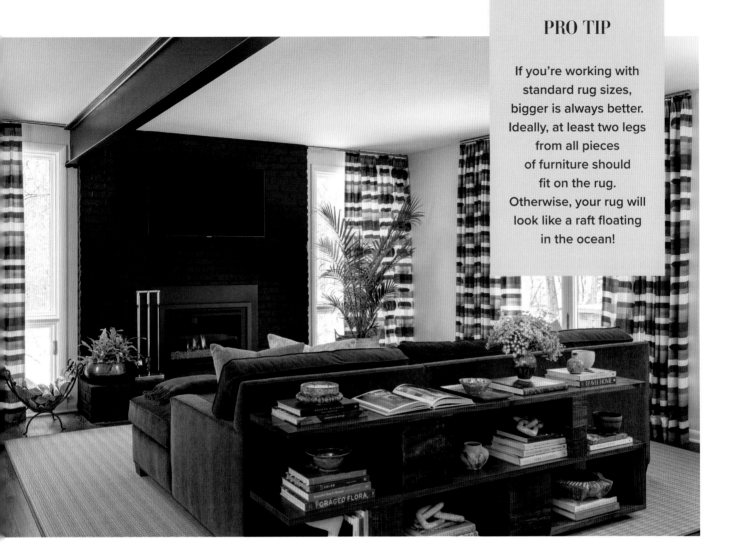

PRO TIP

If you're working with standard rug sizes, bigger is always better. Ideally, at least two legs from all pieces of furniture should fit on the rug. Otherwise, your rug will look like a raft floating in the ocean!

The lounge was the last area to tackle on the main floor. This space was opened up during the kitchen renovation and had several challenges, including an old bar that needed a face-lift and a structural ceiling beam that ran into the middle of the room. First, we painted the ceiling beam black to tie it into the fireplace. Then, we cornered off the area with a sectional to separate it from the kitchen and provide seating for the whole family. Matching draperies tie back to the kitchen color scheme.

The jumping-off point for the kitchen was the graphic navy backsplash tile. The wall is visible from just about every room in the house, so we wanted something dramatic. To keep things light and modern, we selected white quartz countertops and a light brown cabinet color. The large peninsula island was designed with a dual purpose: to seat the maximum number of people and to serve as a divider between the kitchen and the nearby family room.

OPPOSITE: The large window butting up to the island provided plenty of light but looked bare, so we added a Roman shade valance to tie in the family room colors.

ABOVE: We opted to paint the existing bar in a soft fern green, which offsets the mirrored backsplash without being too loud.

OVERLEAF: It was so much fun to design a nursery again. We used a gender neutral jungle-themed mural with a starry blue sky to offset the asymmetrical vaulted ceiling.

DESIGN LESSON
Rugs—The Base Layer

Rugs are often an afterthought when designing a room. People frequently order all their soft seating and only then turn their attention to the rug. In most circumstances, it is best to determine the size of the rug first, as the rug can—and should—dictate the floor plan and traffic flow.

Ideally, you want a rug that will fit all the furniture you've selected for your room.

- A family room rug should be 4–6 inches larger than the furniture footprint of the sofa or sectional, chairs, end tables, and ottoman or coffee table.
- The dining room rug needs to be 24–36 inches larger on all sides than the table and chairs.
- A bedroom rug should be 4–6 inches larger than the furniture footprint of the bed, nightstands, and bench at the foot of bed.

When purchasing a rug for any space in your house, consider the material and the rug's construction.

- Wool rugs are best for durability and softness.
- Wool and nylon blends are great for kids and pets.
- Polypropylene is best for durability and can be outdoors.
- Jute is a great option if you want a natural fiber, but it does stain and show water marks if it gets wet.
- Silk is very soft and beautiful, but not good in high traffic areas.

PHILLIPS CABIN

FAMILY RETREAT

I love when a previous client calls with a new project. This was my fourth house for this family of eight from Columbus, Ohio, and in many ways, the most fun. Their vision was a weekend retreat within driving distance of their main residence, a home that could serve as a gathering place for older kids in college and younger kids still at home.

Nestled in the rolling hills of central Ohio, this picturesque cabin was the perfect spot. A long, winding, gravel driveway ushers guests through a certified arboretum to the main house. The sprawling, eleven-acre property has two separate structures: the main house and a small cottage constructed in the same likeness, located a hundred yards away. Although built in 2018, both the main cabin and cottage are integrated into the landscape and look as if they've been there forever. The driveway loops from the main house to the cottage.

BENJAMIN MOORE PAINT COLORS, FROM TOP: Orange Parrot 2169-20, Hunter Green 2041-10, Seaside Resort 725, Pale Smoke 1584, Wrought Iron 2124-10, Odessa Pink HC - 59, Prussian Blue CW-625.

PRO TIP

If you don't have room for a large sectional or don't like this look, try one long sofa with two lounge chairs or love seats to achieve a similar function.

One of the most distinctive features of the house—and the most challenging—was the completely open living room. Grounded by an enormous stone fireplace, the massive space with concrete floors was intimidating.

I always like to begin with the function of the space and how the family intends to utilize the room. In this case, they really wanted a place to spend time together. With a family of eight, that meant creating three spaces where the family could gather: a game area, a TV-watching area, and a dining-conversation area.

As with most farmhouses, there was a lot of wood: on the ceilings, wood beams, doors, and casing. While wood creates warmth, it can be dark and feel heavy. To combat this feeling, we ran a gorgeous, blue-gray textured paper on all the walls throughout the main area except the fireplace wall. We kept the existing rustic chandelier in the center of the house but added two custom-colored barn-red lanterns at either end.

Just inside the entry we added a large round table, five comfortable chairs, and a bookcase to make the perfect spot to play games or cards or build puzzles.

DESIGN LESSON

How to Create a Flow

When you're planning furniture for any space, the first thing you need to do is identify traffic patterns: How does someone walk through the room? In what direction? From there, create walkways (the areas where you move through the room). Generally, we like to leave 36 inches for a walkway, but if you are limited on space, 32 inches is adequate. Visually block off this space; think of it as a no-go zone. Don't put furniture or anything else that might interfere with the traffic flow in this area.

OPPOSITE: We added colorful vintage rugs to lift the heaviness created by the dark and substantial island.

The inspiration for the kitchen was a Cole & Son Arance Orange/Cream wallpaper, which brought just the right amount of playfulness and color to give the wood-heavy space new life. I wanted to add contrast to the neutral cabinets and countertops, so we selected a textured vinyl wallpaper in a tangerine color for the remaining walls. The existing kitchen island—a former printing press table with an antique marble top—was a bonus. I wanted to preserve this unconventional, reclaimed beauty as a centerpiece of the space.

The screened-in porch adjacent to a secondary dining area was difficult because, while the clients wanted a comfortable place to relax, the space was open to the elements. With the use of quality outdoor furniture, we treated the porch as you would any other indoor room. We united the dining and secondary living area with an indoor-outdoor rug, connecting the spaces and giving it a cohesive feel.

RIGHT: We used four chairs instead of a sectional or two sofas here to maximize flexibility. These chairs can be rearranged easily or pulled into the main family room if needed.

PRO TIP

When there is limited wall space, using one way drapery panels can add color and softness.

ABOVE: The extra-large nightstands anchor the room and provide plenty of surface for lamps, books, phone chargers, and other plug-in items. The bed is upholstered in a fabulous, large-scale, indoor-outdoor fabric to create drama. We flanked the side windows with one-way draw panels in a splashy print for another pattern layer.

OPPOSITE: A textural, blush-toned wallpaper in the en suite bath coordinates with the palette in the bedroom. The embroidered Roman shade pulls in its blues and burgundies.

The cabin has two bedrooms. The main bedroom had a lot of potential, with great light and a pitched ceiling. We decided to wrap the walls in a pale blue vinyl wallpaper (the homeowners' favorite color) and added a unique, organic light fixture. A new take on an old antler-style fixture, the white resin piece adds just the right amount of whimsy and light to the room.

The guest room initially presented a design challenge, as it is located directly outside the dining room and we needed the spaces to flow. To make matters more complicated, its connecting bathroom doubles as the powder room. The previous owners had left a few pieces of furniture, one of them being an iron bed. I decided to keep it and lacquer it in red paint, which became the jumping-off point for this room. Keeping the wallpaper a neutral blue ensured the room flowed easily into the main space.

PULPIT ROCK

HISTORIC CHARM MEETS MODERN LIVING

Every now and again, I feel connected to a place in a way that exceeds the typical design experience. Pulpit Rock is one of those. This Edgeworth, Pennsylvania, structure was built in 1901 by famed architects Rutan and Russell as a vacation home for Samuel C. Walker, whose family owned a Pittsburgh-based brickmaking and refractory company. The house was built using stone quarried from a hill on-site. Walker named the mansion Pulpit Rock because years previous, Native American chiefs would stand on the large rocks located in the front yard to speak to their tribes.

This historic estate was so captivating, it made modern design lovers abandon a custom dream home. I had been working with my clients on designing and building a new, very modern glass-and-steel home when Pulpit Rock went on the market. Although it was the exact opposite of what my clients thought they wanted, they fell in love with the home. With its location on a private hilltop surrounded by trees, it's easy to see why. They purchased the historic mansion and sold the lot where they had been planning to build their modern dream home.

BENJAMIN MOORE PAINT COLORS, FROM TOP: Citron 2024-30, Calypso Blue 727, Crushed Berries 2076-30, Silver Mist 1619, Twilight Blue 2067-30, Green Meadows 2040-20.

However, the clients weren't total historic converts. While they loved the historic home, my clients wanted a modern aesthetic, and, most of all, they wanted color—lots of it. So, we set out on the challenging yet exhilarating task of designing a modern interior for a historic home that would also work for a family with three young children and three dogs.

OPPOSITE AND ABOVE: The first interior design opportunity at Pulpit Rock was actually outside—the expansive covered porch that runs the length of the house. Here we created a conversation area by adding an area rug and modern, low-backed furniture. An outdoor bar cart makes the porch an ideal spot to entertain or to just relax and enjoy the views.

Inside, this very old house has a traditional layout. An enormous center hall welcomes you as you enter the front door, with a large formal living room to the right and a more casual family room to the left. A dramatic, wide staircase is center stage, with incredible, original leaded-glass windows overlooking the backyard. While the bones of the house were amazing, the décor was staid and needed an update.

We started in the center hall, where the client had a vision for a colorful rug to greet guests in the entryway. We chose a large, vintage, overdyed rug in fuchsia. As for wallpaper, we wanted something that would fit in with the natural setting of the home while not reading as boring. We settled on Cole & Son's Woods and Pears in silver/gray. It provides the perfect backdrop for all the wonderful colors to come.

DESIGN LESSON
Think before Tossing

In many instances, an existing item can be reused or repurposed in another location. My mom always said, "If you buy something you love, you'll find a place for it."

• Existing mirrors, chests, and nightstands are prime candidates for painting. Consider painting the frame on an old piece of artwork to modernize it. A few coats of high-shine paint can transform a piece.

• Although reupholstering is not necessarily a budget option (it can be almost as expensive as buying new), covering an old family heirloom with new fabric is one of my favorite ways to personalize a sentimental piece—and it's earth-friendly too.

Don't be afraid to mix and match the old with the new. In the powder room we sanded down and lacquered an old mirror in a soft lilac.

A favorite piece in the house is a clock that belonged to the husband's great-grandfather. This grandfather clock had been passed around the family and no one really wanted it. A dark wood clock certainly did not fit with our vision for the house, but when I suggested we lacquer it a color, everyone got excited! As our color palette for the entry and adjoining living room and family room cemented, we felt that a bright yellow citron would be the perfect complement to the spaces.

As with most rooms where we have more than one seating area, we chose to do one large area rug to anchor the room.

The parlor is the largest space in the house and opens into the dining room, which creates a lot of visual drama but poses a challenge when it comes to design. We needed the two spaces to flow but also have their own identity. Our client fell in love with a colorful ikat-patterned fabric for drapery, which provided an excellent color palette to expand on. Both rooms had a chair rail running around the perimeter, so we selected a beautiful hand-dyed wallpaper to unite the two spaces. We painted the walls a very pale lilac to round out the space.

The furniture layout also proved to be difficult, as we wanted to maintain traffic flow for walking while making the room feel cozy and providing enough seating for entertaining. Because the parlor is longer than it is wide, we decided to split the room into two separate seating areas. Flanking the fireplace, we placed a one-arm chaise longue opposite two lounge chairs. A large, low ottoman sits between the seating areas to serve as a coffee table. We then floated a midsize sofa with its back to the entryway with a beautifully shaped ottoman in front.

PRO TIP

Anytime you are walking into the back of a sofa, it is best to keep the sofa height to 32 inches or lower to keep the room feeling open.

The existing chandelier was extremely formal and too flashy for the style of the room, so we replaced it with a clean, modern fixture.

Since the dining room is open to the parlor, we used the same wall treatment (lilac paint above the chair rail and hand-dyed wallpaper below). A very large live-edge table was already in the space, so we needed to find a way to inject color and excitement into the room. Enter a one-of-a-kind abstract rug, turquoise lacquered finish on the mirrored built-ins, a shimmery mica wallpaper for the ceiling, and lollipop-colored chairs around the table.

We paired the neon citron wallpaper with two custom ottomans covered in a lively chevron pattern to pull it all together The husband, an avid gardener, keeps many of his plants in this room, which makes it feel magical.

Just off the dining room is the sunroom, which has floor-to-ceiling windows and the most incredible tiled floor. We didn't want to do too much to this room, as it was so beautiful already. But, since you can see a sliver of it from the front door, I wanted to use some color. We took a chance with neon citron, textured wallpaper, and it paid off! One of my favorite spaces in the house, it is clean, bright, and appealing.

While the stone porch creates another "room" outside, it also significantly darkens the family room. Despite having a large bank of windows, this space always felt dim. Sometimes I find it's best to just go with the moodiness of a space versus trying to make it something it isn't. In this case, we decided to lacquer the ceiling cobalt blue. The reflection of the light coming in from the windows creates the most incredible hue and draws the eye upwards. We complemented the ceiling color with a large vintage overdyed rug in the same shade of blue.

PRO TIP

An easy and affordable way to make a big statement in a space is to paint the doors, trim, and even the ceiling. Pick an unusual color to create excitement.

BILL CUNNINGHAM

New Classic

KATE MOSS

OPPOSITE: Off the sitting area is a small breakfast nook framed in the same signature stone that's found throughout the house. The nook presented a bit of a challenge because it was such a small space with very few walls, but I really wanted this space to pop! Ultimately, we decided to use the ceiling in the room, as it had the most real estate. We chose a large-scale, abstract grass cloth and wrapped the ceiling and slivers of wall in the paper to create a breakfast box full of color.

The kitchen had a lot of great existing details to work with. A marble-topped island centers the space, and the ceiling enhanced with antique tin. We decided to swap out the lighting first, which made a huge difference. We replaced the existing traditional chandelier with a white resin fixture and swapped out the sconces for modern crystal ones that added just the right amount of glam. The existing stone in this space added a lot of texture, while the blue-and-white-striped grass cloth wallpaper opposite the island was the perfect jumping off spot for the kitchen and sitting area color scheme.

Whenever possible, I try to capture the personalities of my clients with personal details. This couple is avid Grateful Dead fans and have traveled the country to see the band play over the years. So, when it came to the main bedroom, we decided to frame their favorite Dead posters for the wall and selected six that reflected both colors in the room and their favorite shows. At the last minute, I decided to paint the built-ins. We needed to balance the excitement of the other side of the room, and a bold, lush shade of green did just that.

All houses, no matter how wonderful, have limitations. One of the challenges with this house was closet space. The wife worked in fashion in New York City before moving to Pittsburgh and had no shortage of clothing, shoes, and bags. The main bedroom had only a very small, shared closet, After debating several different options, we decided to convert an existing guest room across the hall into her closet. She really wanted something functional and dramatic as a backdrop for all her treasures. I chose a very dark charcoal gray for the walls, as the room had tons of light. But we still needed the drama factor—thus, a mirrored trellis wallpaper on the ceiling.

We also repurposed the existing, and much too fancy, chandelier from the dining room in the swanky closet on the second floor. It's amazing how a piece can have such just the right effect in a different space.

The homeowners wanted a space where the kids and dogs could hang out without having to worry about stains. A large stone fireplace across from the kitchen island proved just the spot. We created a sitting area with a set of lounge chairs covered in a colorful geometric pattern and added a neutral indoor-outdoor rug to ground the room. Splashes of color in large-scale abstract painting by local Pittsburgh artist Mia Tarducci add a jolt of fun to the space.

DESIGN LESSON

Express Yourself with Color

Selecting the right color palette for any space is essential. To begin, choose colors you are drawn to, but don't be afraid to add a pop of something outside of your comfort zone. If you're feeling hesitant, experiment with a pillow or a throw that can be easily replaced. Here is a breakdown of color families to get you started:

HIGH CONTRAST NEUTRALS

Neutrals are particularly effective when paired together or with high-contrast colors. Black and white, navy and cream, deep green and beige are great combinations.

MEDIUM BRIGHTS

Medium brights are my favorite color palette. This range of colors allows you to move in just about any direction without having to worry about anything clashing. Medium brights can also be paired with black and white to create space and balance.

PASTELS

Pastels can be beautiful but are often considered too feminine. One of my favorite techniques is to use a soft pastel paired with dark grays and navy blues to provide masculinity, sophistication, and balance.

RABBIT HILL

ART COLLECTOR'S HAVEN

Built in the late 1800s, Rabbit Hill is a special historic site in the Sewickley Valley. The Victorian-style home was due for a kitchen update, and a leaky dishwasher was the catalyst for the clients to contact me for help. Though the project began as a kitchen renovation, it grew and grew. We were lucky to have incredible clients who trusted us with key decisions and let us reimagine the first floor of this beautiful home. Designed around the owners' vast and impressive art collection, this home is one of my all-time favorites. It was so much fun to pull colors from the artwork and coordinate them with bold patterns. The result is a rich, layered look that's wholly unique to its owners.

BENJAMIN MOORE PAINT COLORS, FROM TOP: Peacock Feathers 724, Denim Wash 838, Storm AF 700, Rosy Tan 2091-50, Royal Fuchsia 2078-30, Majestic Blue 2051-40.

PRO TIP

If you have a large front hall, don't be afraid to furnish it! Add a pair of chairs or an upholstered bench.

The foyer had an original black-and-white marble checkerboard floor with a dark green border. We balanced it with a large-scale floral wallpaper that gives light and levity and makes for a dramatic first impression. We installed a small-scale animal print runner for the entire three-story staircase and painted the stair rails (once a harsh black) a soft gray to complement the floor and wallpaper.

Initially the clients wanted to replace the original floor, but I felt strongly that the classic marble design was inherent to the charm of the house. After considering a few possible replacement options, the homeowners decided that keeping the marble was the right thing to do.

I selected a large-scale floral wallpaper to soften the space, allow for graphic balance, and give an anchor to the tall ceilings. A long console adds warmth (and a place to drop keys and mail), while modern sconces and pearl-inlaid benches with playful upholstery give the room some layers—and a bit of an edge. An oversize, modern chandelier is the perfect topper to the dramatic space.

OPPOSITE: Colors from the front hall flow into the family room, where artwork abounds.

RIGHT: The drapery pulls from the colors of the artwork, but in a playful, abstract way, tying the room together without being too obvious.

DESIGN LESSON

How to Make the Most
OF A NARROW ROOM

Along with all the character, most older homes come with oddly shaped rooms that often have unusual dimensions. If you're faced with a long, narrow room, my advice is:

- Float your seating arrangement in the middle of the room. If you place the sofa or sectional crosswise, it visually pushes the walls outward, making the room seem wider.
- Divide the room into two separate zones but keep them united with one large rug. Consider two conversation areas or a TV-watching area and a game area.
- Create an art wall to draw the eye upward.
- Use circular items to break up the long, straight lines of a narrow room. A round ottoman and round light fixtures and lampshades will soften the space.

To the right of the entry hall is a generously sized living room. A previous addition had split the room into two halves. The closer half of the room had a lower ceiling and an entry to the kitchen beside an oddly off-centered fireplace. The center of the room was marked by the original curved bulkhead, and the back half of the room had a higher ceiling. The homeowners had no idea what to do with this room, so it was rarely used.

This room presented a design challenge because of its length and the need to satisfy two functions: The clients wanted to be able to relax and watch TV here, or enjoy a meal or play a board game. We opted to unify the two rooms by hanging identical light fixtures at matching heights in both areas. One large rug also helps tie together the two spaces. We selected the color palette in the living room in conjunction with the homeowners' bright and vibrant art collection.

Down a short hallway to the kitchen,
guests are greeted by an oversize marble
island and bold light fixtures that meet the
scale of the island, provide more light for
the space, and take advantage of the tall
ceilings.

Because everyone ends up congregating in the kitchen, the homeowners opted for a large bonus seating area instead of a dining table and chairs. The centerpiece of the room is a nearly six-foot, sixteen-globe floating chandelier. The clients wanted a light fixture that was more of a sculptural element—and this certainly is. A soft blue chenille sofa and two swivel chairs covered in outdoor fabric are offset by a bold ikat drapery.

PREVIOUS PAGE RIGHT: The dining room is a place for drama! Pairing a modern paper with traditional moldings epitomizes the home's antique-meets-new sensibility.

RIGHT: A mix of texture, pattern, and color make the study a visually appealing yet comfortable workspace.

OVERLEAF: To soften the study windows, we added drapery panels in a large-scale abstract tree print fabric.

Back through the front hall and to the right is the study. There we found very large cracks in the walls. Instead of taking on major repairs, we decided to use a commercial grade vinyl on the walls. I selected a dark charcoal wall covering to create an unexpected backdrop for the artwork they planned to hang. Not only does it look great, but it also adds drama and makes the space feel cozy. The paper gives a lot more depth than a white gallery wall.

DESIGN LESSON

Wall of Art

Most of us have artwork lurking in our basement or in a closet somewhere. Whether inherited or items that have lost their appeal due to a dated frame, reframing is an excellent way to reinvent artwork and create a space that you will love. While it can seem intimidating to know where to begin, I recommend just diving in.

- Start with the largest piece first and work your way around the wall from there.
- It's often unclear what will look best until you start hanging, and decisions can be made on the fly—it's just a nail that can easily be moved higher or lower if need be.
- Simple black frames can be purchased just about anywhere and work especially well when going for the "gallery wall" look.
- Likewise, don't be afraid to mix and match different styles of frames; old with new.

ROSE LANE

CLASSIC WITH A TWIST

This charming 1898 Victorian, which is rumored to have been part of the underground railroad, sits sideways tucked down a private lane. My mom and I had worked on the house together years earlier, and it was time for an update. The clients have always been true to the style and history of the house but wanted it to work for modern living. Mixing new with old means the home can keep much of its original character.

Our clients wanted to renovate and expand the existing kitchen, tweak the family room, and completely redesign the living room. Older homes have often undergone prior renovations—which can present some challenges—and this project was no exception. Several columns had been positioned in the middle of the main side entrance, making it impossible to utilize this area in any meaningful way. We were able to remove all but one column, opening the space to create a bar on the back wall.

BENJAMIN MOORE PAINT COLORS, FROM TOP: Peacock Feathers 724, Denim Wash 838, Storm AF 700, Rosy Tan 2091-50, Royal Fuchsia 2078-30, Majestic Blue 2051-40.

To revive what had once been a dark space with limited access, we redesigned the bar to showcase a handmade verdigris tile backsplash. Cantilevered, thick glass shelves are flanked by a pair of double brass sconces. A colorful vintage rug and a navy-blue cabinet base with handmade chunky hardware complete the space. Such details can completely change the feel of an entire space.

OPPOSITE: Hanging sconces affixed above the tops of the windows and matching globes with brass accents ground the huge island.

Removing the columns also opened up the kitchen, allowing for considerably more island seating and a better view to the large windows overlooking the side yard. The husband, an accomplished chef, wanted more prep space, so we decided to push out and expand the footprint several feet to accommodate a larger island and more room for traffic flow. The couple both come from large families and big Sunday-night dinners are a regular affair. The expansion also gave us the opportunity to incorporate five new large windows where there had once been a brick wall.

PRO TIP

To create a unique
and refined look for
the kitchen, continue
tile to the ceiling and
around windows.

The family room was the result of an earlier renovation and was saddled with several challenges, the greatest of which was an existing wraparound porch that limited our ability to expand the room by more than two feet. We played around with different floor plans and ultimately decided to expand the bay window by two feet to accommodate two small swivel chairs in a complementary color. A love seat and chaise face one another for optimal TV watching, and an oversize ottoman covered in an animal-print outdoor fabric acts as a coffee table.

A grand front entry (next page) with a formal split staircase lies just beyond the new kitchen area. Pairing a modern paper with traditional moldings epitomizes the home's antique-meets-new sensibility. Like many of the older homes in this area, the front of the house faces the original railroad tracks that, over time, became the highway. The neighborhood roads and private driveway were built later and lead to the side and back of the house.

OVERLEAF: The front door hadn't been used in years, so we decided to utilize the ample floor space as an additional seating area. A beaded, tone-on-tone, geometric wallpaper modernizes and lightens the space, while an animal-print carpet anchors slipper chairs covered in a multicolor woven.

The formal living room was one of the last rooms that my mom and I had worked on together, so it was nostalgic to be here again. The clients still loved the room but wanted an update. There were quite a few bookcases and a favorite painting the couple wanted to keep, so we started there, adding a gorgeous, Scandinavian-style custom rug in various shades of blue and gray to complement the artwork.

Due to the size of the family room and the ever-expanding needs of the family, we opted to redesign the living room with an added television in mind. The built-in bench had long gone unused, and with its proximity to the fireplace, we wanted to make it more functional. We added an oval table and a pair of backless stools for more seating, making room for the whole family.

OPPOSITE: Textured gray-blue wallpaper lends a soft feel, and a tailored Roman shade with tuxedo trim elevates the level of detail.

ABOVE: The backs of the bookcases pop with a deep purple, hummingbird wallpaper.

DESIGN LESSON

Ottoman or Coffee Table?

An ottoman or coffee table is necessary in any family room, both for function and to complete the room.

No matter what style you choose—the most important factor in an ottoman or coffee table is height. Your ottoman or coffee table should be 1 to 3 inches lower than the furniture around it, or around 16 to 17 inches in height. Your ottoman or coffee table can never be too low—but having it too high is a big mistake. It's not functional and looks out of place.

You should allow 14 inches between the sofa and the ottoman or coffee table for walking space.

Ottomans and coffee tables serve different purposes:

Go for an ottoman if . . .
you like to put your feet up and relax. Most people find it uncomfortable to put their feet on a hard surface for any length of time. A large tray can be placed on any ottoman for drinks, food, etc.

Go for a coffee table if . . .
you want to display items, or plan to eat there or play board games. Coffee tables provide an array of options to express your personal style.

Traffic patterns and size and shape of the room will help determine the shape of the ottoman or coffee table:

- A round or square table works best when there is space to extend out into the room and service other furniture.
- A rectangle is best when there is limited space, or you need to maintain a walkway in front of a seating arrangement.

WINTER COVE

SANCTUARY BY THE SEA

As unexpected projects go, this one takes the cake. A longtime client approached me about helping them renovate and add on to an existing home on the ocean in Blue Hill, Maine. I had to think about it for only about five seconds . . . um, yes!

The setting was spectacular. The house just needed some updates, some new threads, and a small addition. The owners wanted a calm, peaceful (but functional) spot to relax with friends and family. We teamed up with a phenomenal local architect and builder for the structural changes and set out to transform the 1970s structure into a modern-day sanctuary by the sea.

Most visitors enter the house via a side entry, where a custom, circular, cypress staircase links the original mudroom to the new guest suite. A patterned floor tile provides durability, while a soft blue cloud wallpaper provides the right ambience. Custom benches upholstered in outdoor fabric flank the door.

BENJAMIN MOORE PAINT COLORS, FROM TOP: Santorini Blue 1634, Smokestack Gray 2131-40, Pink Moiré 050, Gray Sky 2131-70, Violet Stone 2069-40, Liberty Park 487.

PREVIOUS OVERLEAF AND OPPOSITE: The guest suite off the circular staircase is a lesson in hospitality. No detail was spared when considering the comfort of guests in this space. We added bold wallpaper and a useful desk in the hallway that leads to the bedroom area. The custom king-size bed is covered in a plaid fabric. Two large nightstands double as storage chests for guests' belongings. The restful color palette continues here with lilac, tan, and cream patterns.

ABOVE: Off the guest bedroom is a living area complete with a sectional and TV, welcoming guests to relax on their own. Our design started with a navy-and-lilac linen drapery, which sets the tone for the room. At the rear of the space, we swathed the angled ceiling in cypress to create a nook for a functional kitchenette with a sink, dishwasher, and refrigerator.

OPPOSITE: The second guest room is dubbed the Peacock Room for the fabulous toile draperies that inspired the magenta and lavender color palette. We used an embroidered chevron pattern on the bed frame. A Lucite bench covered in an ombré velvet stripe provides a surprising modern touch, while two Ming-style occasional chairs bring a traditional element.

ABOVE: The ocean-facing guest room has great light. The wife, an avid gardener, really wanted the room to reflect its outdoor surroundings, so we selected a fresh delphinium print for the drapery. A fun velvet houndstooth on the custom bed frame anchors the wall without windows. Swing arm sconces and metallic end tables add a bit of glam.

LEFT: From the side entry, a long hallway leads to two more guest rooms and this powder room.

The guest hallway leads to the kitchen, dining, and family space.
The original kitchen was quite functional, but it needed an
update, which we accomplished by painting the cabinets and
replacing the countertops for a simple, cost-effective solution.

ABOVE: Cluster tables in front of the dining room couch can be pulled apart for coffee or hors d'oeuvres when entertaining.

RIGHT: We had a large, custom, solid oak table with pedestals made to maximize seating and flanked it with colorful host chairs. Gold-coated orange peels make a simple art installation to enhance the tree wallpaper.

We completely gutted the living room to allow for a vaulted ceiling of lime-washed pine and matching beams. The room's focal point is a fireplace with a depressed slab to showcase a commissioned artwork by Hiroko Takeda. Travertine from the hearth continues onto an integrated stone bar top beside it.

With such a large space, we needed to create a floor plan with enough seating to fill the space while allowing for views of the ocean. We went with matching custom sofas that we placed back-to-back to separate the room and create two distinct seating areas—one to look out to the view of the ocean and the other to surround the fireplace area. The client wanted the room to be calm and natural like the surroundings, so we mixed soft patterns and solids in grays, blush, lavenders, and blues to warm the vast space.

We kept things fresh in the screened porch area, extending the soft colors of the living room. A bold lantern grounds the space.

I wanted the study to be more masculine but still light, so we created all-new millwork and paneling, which we painted a soft cream. We dressed the windows in a smart navy-and-beige print and added colorful runners, which lead to the main suite.

OPPOSITE: We expanded the main bath to include his and hers spaces in an open-concept layout. The peninsula approach provides separate accommodations that face one another, with backlit mirrors suspended from the ceiling. Birdseye maple cabinetry is topped with Danby marble from Vermont.

ABOVE: A comfy chaise longue sits next to the walk-in shower and tub for reading and relaxing. Most people shy away from furniture in the bathroom, but it makes a lot of sense to have a place to curl up in such a personal space.

DESIGN LESSON

Where to Splurge!

Whether you are decorating your whole house or just one room, chances are you don't have or want to spend unlimited funds. There are some areas where it makes sense to save and other areas that are worth the investment. Here are some places I think give the biggest bang for your buck:

- Custom drapery not only provides a high-end look, but it also helps personalize any space and provides a great backdrop for color.

- A good rug that is large enough so all the furniture pieces can have at least some legs resting on it helps finish the room and is a worthwhile investment.

- Properly scaled, quality furniture is critical for both look and function.

- Antiques and one-of-a-kind pieces, like a console, can anchor a room.

- Lighting can make or break a space. Don't be afraid to invest in a larger scale statement chandelier.

- Performance and heavy-duty upholstery textiles are well worth the extra cost. They will take the wear and tear and help furniture last longer.

- Wallpaper creates interest, whether used in the entire room or just behind a bookcase.

- Artwork is always worth the investment. Years later, you can move a piece to another room or change the frame and make it new again.

- Lamps both finish and provide a visual element to any room —even if there is overhead lighting.

SOURCES

ARTWORK AND ACCESSORIES

ALL ACROSS AFRICA
100 W 35th St, Ste G
National City, CA 91950

ANNE IRWIN FINE ART
690 Miami Circle NE
Atlanta, GA 30324

ANTHROPOLOGIE HOME
5000 South Broad St, Bldg 18
Philadelphia, PA 19112

BE GALLERIES
3583 Butler St
Pittsburgh, PA 15201

CHAIRISH CO
465 California St, Ste 1250
San Francisco, CA 94104

GRANT WIGGINS
Tempe, AZ

HIROKO TAKEDA STUDIO
232 Third St
Brooklyn, NY 11215

JAMIE YOUNG CO
331 West Victoria St
Gardena, CA 90745

JONATHAN ADLER ENTERPRISES
333 Hudson St, Fl 7
New York, NY 10013

JOWDY STUDIO
7800 Susquehanna St, Ste 203
Pittsburgh, PA 15208

MIA TARDUCCI
7800 Susquehanna St
Pittsburgh, PA 15208

NICOLE RENEE RYAN ART STUDIO
209 S Pitt St
Mercer, PA 16137

THOMAS FUCHS CREATIVE
1541 Brickell Ave, Ste 3401
Miami, FL 33129

BEDDING

EASTERN ACCENTS
4201 W Belmont Ave
Chicago, IL 60641

JOHN ROBSHAW HOME
245 W 29th St
New York, NY 10001

PIONEER LINENS
210 N Clematis St
West Palm Beach, FL 33401

MATOUK
925 Airport Rd
Fall River, MA 02720

WILLIAMS SONOMA, INC.
75 Front St
Brooklyn, NY 11201

CARPETING AND RUGS

ABC CARPET AND HOME
888 Broadway
New York, NY 10003

BOKARA RUG COMPANY
50 Enterprise Ave N
Secaucus, NJ 07094

CREATIVE TOUCH RUGS
6 Washington Ave
Fairfield, NJ 07004

FJ KASHANIAN RUGS
21 W Mall
Plainview, NY 11803

HEIRLOOMS VINTAGE RUGS
3701 S Dixie Hwy
West Palm Beach, FL 33405

RUG AND KILIM
240 East 59th Street
New York, NY 10022

SADDLEMANS
17307 Mt. Wynne Cir
Fountain Valley, CA 92708

SARAH BUMGARDNER
Bar Harbour, ME

STARK CARPET
979 3rd Ave, FL 11
New York, NY 10022

FURNITURE AND CASE GOODS

ANDREU WORLD
200 Lexington Ave, Ste 111
New York, NY 10016

CAMERICH USA
PO Box 390
Renton, WA 98057

CENTURY FURNITURE
PO BOX 608
Hickory, NC 28603

CUSTOM FURNITURE, LA
13930 S Figueroa St
Los Angeles, CA 90061

FOUR HANDS
2090 Woodward St
Austin, TX 78744

JANUS ET CIE
8687 Melrose Ave, Ste B193
West Hollywood, CA 90069

JOHN MALECKI
Pittsburgh, PA

JULIAN CHICHESTER
200 Lexington Ave, Ste 604
New York, NY 10016

MADE GOODS
918 S Stimson Ave
City of Industry, CA 91745

PALECEK
601 Parr Blvd
Richmond, CA 94801

PHILLIPS COLLECTION
916 Finch Ave
High Point, NC 27263

PORT ELIOT
211 Howard St
Greenwood, MS 38930

TRITTER FEEFER
PO Box 4500
LaGrange, GA 30241

VILLA & HOUSE
95 Mayhill St, Ste 5
Saddle Brook, NJ, 07663

LIGHTING

ARTERIORS HOME
1413 Dragon St
Dallas, TX 75207

BOYD LIGHTING
375 Potrero Ave
San Francisco, CA 94103

IRONWARE INTERNATIONAL
2421 Cruzen St
Nashville, TN 37211

LINDSEY ADLEMAN STUDIO
324 Lafayette St, 7th Fl
New York, NY 10012

PORTA ROMANA
Chelsea Harbour
London SW1 0OXE

STONEGATE DESIGNS
2345 N Ernie Krueger Cir
Waukegan, IL 60087

THE NATURAL LIGHT
PO Box 16449
Panama City, FL 32406

VAUGHAN LIGHTING
979 3rd Ave, Ste 1511
New York, NY 10022

VISO LIGHTING
388 Carlaw Ave
Toronto, ON M4M 2T4

VISUAL COMFORT
22400 Northwest Lake Dr
Houston, TX 77095

URBAN ELECTRIC
2120 Noisette Blvd
North Charleston, SC 29405

FABRICS AND WALLCOVERINGS

ARTE USA, INC
1000 Cobb Place Blvd, Ste 220
Kennesaw, GA 30144

LA CASAMANCE
93 Rue Des Moines
75017, Paris, Île de France

CHEZ SHEA DESIGNS
Atlanta, GA

CLARENCE HOUSE
979 Third Ave, Ste 205
New York, NY 10022

COLE & SON
199 Eade Road
London, N4 1DN, UK

COWTAN & TOUT
148 39th St
Brooklyn, NY 11232

ELITIS, INC.
2 Bis rue Jean Rodier
31400 Toulouse, FR

F. SCHUMACHER & CO
979 Third Ave, Ste 832
New York, NY 10022

FABRICUT
9303 E 46th St
Tulsa, OK 74145

JIM THOMPSON
351 Peachtree Hills Ave
Atlanta, GA 30305

LAURA PARK DESIGNS
1033 Providence Rd
Charlotte, NC 28207

KRAVET
250 Crossways Park Dr
Woodbury, NY 11797

MISSONI HOME
676 Madison Ave
New York, NY 10065

OSBORNE & LITTLE
Riverside House
26 Osiers Rd
London, SW18 1NH, UK

PERENNIALS FABRICS
140 Regal Row, #5606
Dallas, TX 75247

PHILLIP JEFFRIES
180 Passaic Ave
Fairfield, NJ 07004

PIERRE FREY
47 Rue de Petits Champs
75001 Paris, FR

PORTER TELEO
5801 Kessler Ln, Ste 201
Shawnee, KS 66203

QUADRILLE WALLPAPER AND FABRICS
979 Third Ave, Ste 1415
New York, NY 10022

ROMO, INC.
16722 West Park Circle Dr
Chagrin Falls, OH 44023

SCALAMANDRÉ
979 Third Ave, Ste 1002
New York, NY 10022

SANDERSON DESIGN GROUP
Chalfont House
Oxford Road
Denham, UB9 4DX, UK

THIBAUT
1095 Morris Ave
Union, NJ 07083

ZOFFANY
Chalfont House
Oxford Road
Uxbridge, UB9 4DX, UK

ACKNOWLEDGMENTS

It takes a village to write an interior design book. I'd like to thank the following people for helping me to achieve this dream:

Ellen Niven and crew for your guidance and for believing in me.

Madge Baird and everyone at Gibbs Smith for giving me this incredible opportunity.

Rita Sowins for the lovely book design.

Hadley Keller and Tori Mellott for all your sage advice and wisdom. Love you both!

SGP and 007 for your continued support. I wouldn't be here without you.

Nick Sargent, Carmel Brantley, Caulin Grant, and Dave Bryce for shooting such beautiful images and for bringing my designs to life.

Lucy Bamman, Erin Swift, Ben Hayes, and Jen Hartman for your helping hands and expert styling.

Tom Kirchhoff for giving me the chance to work with you on KB. I'm so thankful.

Molly Lucas for being my right hand and always giving 110 percent.

Stacey Westwood -Zunic for supporting me both professionally and personally for the last fifteen years. I absolutely could not have done this without you by my side. You are the best!

Caitlin Richter for tracking all the details and staying calm when the rest of us don't.

Flora Hunzeker and Emily Dwyer for being my partners in crime and the best badasses I know.

Trish Ciesinski and Elizabeth Sykes for letting me drag you into my antics.

Jason Leviere for showing up every single time. Brenda and Cliff Hayes for working your magic.

Savannah Sexton and Nicky Slowinski for holding down the fort and keeping our household running smoothly through all the madness that is my life.

My family, especially Susan Brown, Roger Wiegand, and Mel and Marilyn Wentz, for all your love and support.

Jack, Cooper, Finn, and Marlowe for being my biggest cheerleaders and for letting me be yours. You are my heart.

Chris, my wonderful husband, I'm so grateful for everything you do for us. Thanks for always having my back. Your continued support means everything to me.

A special thank-you to all my clients, who have become my dear friends. Thank you for trusting me with your designs and for allowing me to invade your personal spaces with lights, cameras, people, food, books, props, plants, and so many flowers. I am forever grateful.

Finally, to my mom, Kay, who shaped my love for design and taught me everything she knew. She colored this world with kindness. She was gone too soon, but I know she's watching it all and smiling down.

Love you forever—xx